THROUGH
THEIR EYES

POEMS FROM THE UK

Edited By Jess Giaffreda

First published in Great Britain in 2020 by:

Young Writers
Remus House
Coltsfoot Drive
Peterborough
PE2 9BF
Telephone: 01733 890066
Website: www.youngwriters.co.uk

Printed and bound in the UK by BookPrintingUK
Website: www.bookprintinguk.com
YB0433H

FOREWORD

Since 1991, here at Young Writers we have celebrated the awesome power of creative writing, especially in young adults, where it can serve as a vital method of expressing strong (and sometimes difficult) emotions, a conduit to develop empathy, and a safe, non-judgemental place to explore one's own place in the world. With every poem we see the effort and thought that each pupil published in this book has put into their work and by creating this anthology we hope to encourage them further with the ultimate goal of sparking a life-long love of writing.

Through Their Eyes challenged young writers to open their minds and pen bold, powerful poems from the points-of-view of any person or concept they could imagine – from celebrities and politicians to animals and inanimate objects, or even just to give us a glimpse of the world as they experience it. The result is this fierce collection of poetry that by turns questions injustice, imagines the innermost thoughts of influential figures or simply has fun.

The nature of the topic means that contentious or controversial figures may have been chosen as the narrators, and as such some poems may contain views or thoughts that, although may represent those of the person being written about, by no means reflect the opinions or feelings of either the author or us here at Young Writers.

We encourage young writers to express themselves and address subjects that matter to them, which sometimes means writing about sensitive or difficult topics. If you have been affected by any issues raised in this book, details on where to find help can be found at *www.youngwriters.co.uk/info/other/contact-lines*

CONTENTS

Boroughmuir High School, Edinburgh

Phoebe Pryce (14)   1

Diss High School, Diss

Chelsey Bennett (13)   3
Lucia Marquez O'Brien (12)   4
Ruby Aldous (11)   6
Reece Oates (11)   8
Santiago Robles-Hewson (12)   10
Maya Dubiel (11)   12
Ella Rose Osborn (13)   13
Eleanor May Moles (11)   14
Zach Murphy (12)   16
Spencer Jacob Brown (13)   18
Holly Fry (12)   19
Daisy Stubbs (11)   20
Freddie Wimshurst (11)   21
Fleur Court (12)   22
Holly Sutton (12)   24
Ellis White (13)   25
Laurie Shaw (11)   26
Hamish Teare (12)   27
Gracie King (11)   28
Aidan Patrick Quinnan (11)   29
Tia Reed-Hall (12)   30
Solomon Marcks (13)   31
Ellie Victoria Mitchell (11)   32
George Alexander McCathie (11)   33
Hallee Mai Watson (11)   34
Owen Holmes (11)   35
Logan Cobb (13)   36
Katie Weedon (12)   37
Alfie Burr (12)   38

Gabriella Valcsak (12)   39
Ava Niamh Etchells (11)   40
Holly Davey (11)   41
Josh Amey (12)   42
Ellie-Mae Blades (11)   43
Amelia Smith (11)   44
Tori Smith (11)   45
Mia Worby (11)   46
Grace Henderson (12)   47

Honley High School, Honley

Evie Newton (11)   48
Benjamin Crosland (11)   51
Daniel Lydall (11)   52
Holly MacGregor (11)   53
John Fox Gahan (11)   54
Molly Eliza Clarke (11)   55
Lexie Booth (12)   56
Dhaya Haire (11)   57
Amber Eliza Dawson-Spragg (12)   58
Eliza Faye Holroyd (11)   60
Isabella Pickup (11)   61
Molly Brannelly (11)   62
Declan Levay (11)   63
Dylan Thomas Shaw (13)   64
Omar Koroma (13)   65
Charlie David Shaw (11)   66
Kane Eley (12)   67
Jessica Lilley (12)   68
Yousaf Umar Aziz (11)   69
Anayat Yaseen (12)   70
Emily Grace Bradley (11)   71
Emily Lowther (12)   72
Amber Nelmes (13)   73
Leo Jackson (12)   74

Khiara Delgado (11)	75
Ruben Christopher Charles Harrison (11)	76
Eva Tilburn (12)	77
Alex Szoradi (11)	78

Savio Salesian College, Bootle

Faith Murphy Jones (11)	79
Selena Anderson (11)	80

The Oldham Academy North, Royton

Ameera Aslam (11)	81
Cheryl Brown (11)	82
Moezza Asad (13)	84
Sharmin Akthar (13)	85
Masuda Begum (13)	86
Favour Eguasa (13)	88
Anisha Saeed (13)	90
Iza Kauser (11)	91
Fahmida Begum	92
Masuma Begum (13)	93
Ubaid Ullah Sharif Ali-Shanawar (11)	94
Ashleigh-Tashan Alexis Howes (12)	95
Mehedee Hasan Rana (14)	96
Myiesha Hussain (11)	97
Sophia O'Brien (12)	98
Lailah Rahman (13)	99
Caitlin Monk (12)	100
Idrees Saddique (11)	101
Alisha Maybury (13)	102
Donovan Drew Thistleton (14)	103
Mohammed Fahim Hussain (11)	104
Samiha Begum (13)	105
Jessica Nicole Meggison (14)	106
Atiyah Begum (13)	107
Ryan Cropper (11)	108
Luke Hesford (13)	109
Shobnam Yeasmine (11)	110
Jacob Houghton (11)	111
Mia Broadbent (11)	112

Kaif Zahir (11)	113
Sami Chohan (12)	114

Walton High, Walnut Tree

Kadija Diallo	115
George Lashbrook (11)	116
Divya Vasisht (11)	118
Freyja Hawkins	120
Emily Cunningham (12)	122
Jenny Else	123
Sophie Wright (11)	124
Toby Atkinson (12)	125
Oliwia Michalak	126
Jemma Tye	127
Sam Alfie Mounch (12)	128
David Garofil (11)	129
Jorai Ngindu (13)	130
Josh Wicks	131
Lizzy Ann Albans (11)	132
Ella Smith	133
Naeya Mistry	134
Fionnabhair Sarah Filer (13)	135
Shakima Nicholas	136
Ellie Gibson	137

Wester Hailes Education Centre, Edinburgh

Jessica Leeanne Edwards (12)	138
Hannah Millar (11)	139
Emma Burt (12)	140

Wilmington Grammar School For Girls, Dartford

Nina Petryk (13)	141
Lucy Stapley (13)	142
Erin Gardner (13)	143

THE
POEMS

Shadow Of Doubt

I was always with him,
but rarely did he know,
formed on sunny days or by
the winter streetlamps' glow.

Throughout his fateful life,
and when he came to rule,
I watched distorted intentions:
mutated, dreadful, cruel.

His greed was irrepressible,
he crossed the Allies' line,
he dragged his country into war,
condoned atrocious crimes.

He went into hiding,
his final, desperate dare,
even sprawled dead on the floor,
his other half was there.

Did he ever realise,
what he had become?
Whilst I watched on invisible:
helpless, silent, dumb.

Always I despised it,
the power, hate, despair,
yet I was estranged to these
dreams morphed beyond repair.

A shadow is so powerless,
trapped by his violent deeds.
But underneath, my protests,
were seldom more than seeds.

Phoebe Pryce (14)
Boroughmuir High School, Edinburgh

The Black Cloud

They burned a house to dispose of me,
Over a thousand in fact,
Paranoid for my next attack.
Shut the windows and doors,
I will give you a head start,
But truth be told, there is no escape,
My disease will soon reach your heart.
I have an army, you have nothing,
Just submit to your fate,
For I am not bluffing.

You're a snack for me,
My hunger ever growing.
What lies in the future, I can see,
Your body, thrown into the abyss,
For when I am done, you will not be missed.

I am the cloud that brought death,
The blackness that emerged.
I'm the assassin of the night,
I extinguished all the light.
I have many names, you may know me by one,
But you shall know nothing when I'm done.

Now I have tasted you, you are a prisoner to me,
As you have now been sentenced to torment
By your worst nightmare.
The Plague.

Chelsey Bennett (13)
Diss High School, Diss

3

Our Mother

The Earth is our oldest friend,
Our greatest friend,
Our mother, our sister, it keeps us alive.
Literally.
So, explain to me why we are treating Earth
Like she's an enemy?
She has been there for us since forever,
And the way we repay her isn't very clever.
We overdose her with pollution like a drug,
I hear her screams, so why can't you?
Oh, probably because you are the culprit of her murder.
Let me carry on further.
She is the very foundation of human creation.
And you are killing her!
This situation is a very big one.
Too big for children to think they have to handle it.
But they are,
Because you aren't.
It's not rocket science.
It's the Earth's alliance.
In the dark, hand in hand in with our Mother Earth.
And yet she is frightened.
Not of the terrifying emptiness swallowing her up,
But of who she is holding hands with. Us.
She is trembling,
Because our factories are digging deep into her skin,

Drawing blood.
Donald Trump. The King of the Beast.
We are not 'just children,' we are fighters!
Warriors! Believers (Unlike you.)
In one of your extensive speeches you said,
You 'didn't believe in climate change'.
Let me explain it to you.
Let me make you believe.
If a good friend who you have known all your life,
And your parents knew all their lives,
And their parents knew all their lives,
Walked up to you and punched you in the nose,
Would you believe it hurt?
Would you believe there was a reason
Why your oldest friend punched you in the face?
I would believe that too.
So why the hell, are you, a world leader,
Ignoring a punch in the nose from Mother Earth?
I don't know.
What I do know is that you have twelve years
To get your act together
Before all hell breaks loose.
So don't tell us that you don't believe
In climate change,
Or you'll be expecting,
More than a punch in the face.

Lucia Marquez O'Brien (12)
Diss High School, Diss

Deforestation

The sky was clear and blue,
I had just woken up to a day which was new.
The rain from last night has soaked the ground,
Meaning it was muddy all around.
The strange smoke from yesterday had gone,
And all the different birds were singing their own special song.
I climbed down my tree and went for a walk in the morning sun,
As my friends and siblings joined me we began to have lots of fun.
Suddenly, there was a loud bang and the sky flashed red,
Everyone ran away apart from me, it was like they had all gone to bed.
As I looked through the trees I saw men, lots of men,
There was definitely lots more than ten.
They were cutting down the trees,
And with their machines, they were doing it with ease.
Tree after tree fell lifelessly down to the ground,
The whole forest was shaken by the terrible sound.
Unexpectedly a grown man picked me up and dumped me in a cage,
He put the cage on the back of his truck as I began to fill up with rage.
Who do these people think they are destroying my home?
As he drove me away I saw all my brothers and sisters beginning to roam.

I wanted to warn them but luckily they ran away just in time,
Why were these people committing a crime?
When I opened my eyes I was in a zoo,
Well, at least that journey was over as the whole time I felt like I wasn't going to get through.
A few weeks later, I closed my eyes and never opened them again,
That was the end of my life.

Now each time you think of deforestation, you will think of me and how I suffered,
All because my beloved home was destroyed.
Each day more and more trees are getting chopped down killing off all of the animals,
Is there a way we can stop this, just think to see if you can make a change!

Ruby Aldous (11)
Diss High School, Diss

A Dog's Life

I was in a cage with these other dogs.
I was confused and most of all I wanted to get out,
Into a new home, with a comfy bed and a loving owner.
But that's not what happened exactly.
A cold, wet, soggy day,
I was so fed up of all these other annoying dogs.
I hated it, but then it happened.
I widened my eyes,
A small girl with brown eyes,
And her mum walked in.
The girl's face even expressed she wanted a puppy.
I was so nervous but excited at the same time.
The little girl looked up and down,
Her eyes stopped in their tracks,
And stared right into my eyes.
I thought to myself,
This is it. I am finally getting out of here.
She ran as quick as a flash towards her mum.
The girl yanked her hand, "Mum! Mum!" the girl cried out.
"This one mum," she said, "Of course."
They took me out and paid.
I'm out. I'm finally out!
We got to the house, the girl took me up to her room,
And played with me. It was five minutes.
She left me in her room and went downstairs.

I heard mumbling, she came back up and
Took me down. She chucked me outside and locked the
door.
I was sad. I've never felt this way before.
I strolled slowly away and went to find shelter,
Under a cardboard box.
I'll never trust anyone again.

Reece Oates (11)

Diss High School, Diss

The Life Of Hades

As I think of them,
They are destroyed.
It is a tragedy,
But it must be done.

For I am,
The Almighty God,
Hades, God of the Underworld,
God of Destruction.

My brothers won't listen,
My fellow God Thanatos will help,
But it is risky,
Without a doubt.

As I unleash my true form,
They disintegrate into dust,
They run for their lives,
But Kronos' forces won't die that easily.

Thousands of them at least.
We fight for Gods versus Titans,
With my brothers here,
We ought not fail.

They get me down,
And I yell up high!
I am a God and I will never, never die!
I'm filled with hatred beyond power.

I get cut to bits,
With my brother Zeus,
But Poseidon comes,
He will free us.

I am exhausted.
I yell in agony,
As I heal.
This is the life of a God beyond matter.

As I think of what could happen next,
I put on my helmet,
And brass plate armour,
And I walk.

As I go back to war,
Against the Titans,
I think to myself,
A God has never died before...

Until now.

Santiago Robles-Hewson (12)
Diss High School, Diss

My Hospital Bed

As I lie there, motionless in my hospital bed,
The sun shining, children playing,
The birds singing and the wind blowing.
As I lie there, motionless in my hospital bed, laughing,
crying, clapping, I hear,
As I lie there, motionless in my hospital bed.

Mummy, I'm sorry I can't sing with you,
Like you wanted.
Daddy, I'm sorry I can't go fishing with you,
Like you wanted.
Brother, I'm sorry I can't play Lego with you,
Like you wanted.
Sister, I'm sorry I can't bake with you,
Like you wanted,
But I must lie, motionless, on my hospital bed.

I know I won't graduate or drive my first car.
I know I won't ever get married, or have a great job. I know I
won't live a long, beautiful life,
As I must lie, motionless in my hospital bed.

But can I at least, blow out some candles next year?

Maya Dubiel (11)
Diss High School, Diss

Forest Fires

Greta Thunberg

Why are we doing this to the world?
Teenagers and adults too wrapped up in their phones
To care what's going on in this world.
Put them down!
Look what's happening, forests are on fire,
Oceans are being torn apart and destroyed.
The forests are dying,
Ocean animals are crying.
Do something!
I wish people would open their eyes and look,
Look at what they're doing to the world.
Just imagine it for a moment, with all the
Rubbish being thrown on the floor,
In twenty years' time, nothing will be left.
We would have killed our own planet.
Nothing left...
The Amazon Rainforest is on fire and burning,
Down more and more every day. But hey,
Guess what?
You don't care!
Think it through, please?
Do you think this is okay?
Do something, save your world before you destroy it.

Ella Rose Osborn (13)

Diss High School, Diss

Elephants

We all should live to an old age.
But I don't. Not even my family.
We died at a young age,
Because of poachers.

I was born. Then I died.
Because of poachers.
I lived to three.
I was one when poachers came,
And killed my mum and dad,
But they left the bodies,
Took their tusks,
And I was left lonely and sad.

When I was two,
The poachers came back.
I hid in the bushes,
While they killed more of my kind.
The poachers are monsters,
They killed five of my kind,
When they left I came out and I was sad.

When I was three,
They came back,
But I didn't know.
I was drinking.
Then I died.
Because of the poachers.

I was three.
Only three.
I am an elephant.
Almost extinct.
Please save my kind.
I am an elephant.
And I lived till three.

Eleanor May Moles (11)
Diss High School, Diss

Trapped

I did the crime.
I've done my time.
Put it all behind me,
And they won't come and find me.
I want to get a job,
Live a normal life,
Never kill someone with a knife.
I have a criminal record on my CV,
So no one wants to hire me.
One bad comment,
Sent me into a blind rage,
It's like I'm going back a page.
I got sent to the slammer.
It's a real downer.
I'm in death row,
Now I know,
My last meal is soon,
I'll have steak haché,
Eat my ice cream with a spoon.
They call my name to the chair,
It's waiting.
I wonder who else,
Is trapped in this loop,
Doomed to die.
Misery and anger.
I am a danger.

The electricity crackles.
The controllers cackle.
So now I'm waiting,
Waiting to die.

Zach Murphy (12)
Diss High School, Diss

Mirror Of Life

As I see every day,
The beauty of people wash away,
Until you see the truth behind,
You will never understand what's lying, waiting.

Skin sagging down, all the way to the bone.
As life ticks down,
The disguise of happiness that I see all the time,
Makes me wonder if life is misery.

Voices, the sound those things make.
The enigmatic faces stored in my lost and found.
Bring themselves up every once in a while.
I see them and then, and then they are gone,
But they don't say goodbye.

As if I'm not there.
But if you look in a shop or your house,
I am always there.

You look at me and think about
Yourself, always centre of attention.

But who am I, to say...

Since I am only a mirror...

One lonely mirror.

Spencer Jacob Brown (13)
Diss High School, Diss

Everyone Has Feelings

Being who I am, wasn't a choice,
It was a lifestyle.
Hello everybody, my name is anger.
Now you probably know me, or you might not,
But I am a feeling that overpowers you,
Almost every day, this is my story.

Walking down the street,
With only one mission,
To get people to realise,
That everyone has feelings too,
With burning passion all through my body,
The fun was about to begin.

Oh, look a lonely little girl,
Let's go see what is the matter.
No, I'm not going to comfort her,
But just wait to see whether she is worth
Wasting my energy on.

So I wonder, does anyone care?
My eyes lit up with a spark in each corner,
As the lonely little girl began to cry,
But no one stops
To see if she is okay.

Holly Fry (12)
Diss High School, Diss

How Would You Feel?

If you were standing there at your favourite place.
Then suddenly you feel as if someone or something is
watching you.
You freeze not daring to move.
You think run, but you don't dare to.
You make a decision.
Run!
They strike.
Next thing you know, you fall like you're nothing.
More people jump out the bushes with weapons, sharp as
could be.
You feel weak and vulnerable.
You feel as if you're a newborn cub not able to fend for itself
in the wild.
You want to run away and hide from these horrible people.
But you can't!
You feel lifeless.
Suddenly the monsters disappear.
You think they're gone.
But they've taken your horns.
Your most prized possession,
Your pride and joy is gone.
How would you feel?

Daisy Stubbs (11)
Diss High School, Diss

The Jew

As they took Poland, the world changed.
As they took us, we changed.
When we knew where we were going,
We knew what was coming.
A soldier shouted, "Raus aus dem Zug!"
Someone translated it to me, "Get out the train."
He didn't know where we were.
I felt bad, should I tell him?
People got shot, assaulted and killed.
I didn't want to tell him!
All of a sudden, we were in our dorms.
Fear. It hit me. Would I die?
I'm hungry. Everyone looks depressed.
Did they know?
I found the man sobbing.
He found out, the hard way.
He saw the sign that read: *Auschwitz*.
Then he got told, "Geh he die kammern!"
Someone told me they were going to the gas chambers.
I heard shouting and walls being scratched,
Then silence.

Freddie Wimshurst (11)
Diss High School, Diss

Wish I Could Please My Owner

I leap to my owner as I hear the door open.
She picks me up with joy,
Stroking my head,
Playing with my ears,
As I try to lick her, she hugs me,
Letting me know she still loves me.

I bark,
I dance,
Hoping my owner will give me some waffle.
She bends down,
No,
She rubs my back, but not good enough.
As I follow her to eat,
She gives me some waffle,
Yes, thank you.

Why are they leaving me?
I watch.
They say goodbye.
But no reason comes,
I've been left all alone.

Finally, they're back,
I bark with glee.

My darling owner comes,
She picks me up,
Petting me.
Cuddling me.
We are all happy once again.

Fleur Court (12)

Diss High School, Diss

As One Dies Then One Thousand Die

Dropping like flies,
One dies, then one thousand die,
Try looking through the animal's eyes.

I'm an elephant, big and strong,
My tusks are long and special,
Don't act so casual.

I have young of my own,
Needing love and attention,
One dies then another dies.

I'm a proud rhino, with big precious horns,
Don't grind them for money,
I watch around me.

As one dies, then one hundred die.

I run for my life,
Across fields and forests,
Guns are frightening me too much.

I have a herd to look after,
Don't kill me with a weapon,
One dies, then one thousand die.

Stop poaching!

Holly Sutton (12)
Diss High School, Diss

I Am The Forest

I am the forest.
I produce your air and get rid of your pollution,
But still,
You cut me down,
You let me burn.
If you were to let me grow,
The problem would diminish,
But still you persist,
So by all means,
Keep cutting me down,
Keep killing my animals,
Keep burning me alive,
Because when you kill me for your own gain,
You won't hear me screaming,
But believe me when I say,
You'll feel it.
I am the forest,
I produce your air and get rid of your pollution,
But still,
You left me to rot,
You left me to die,
And such is cause and effect.

Ellis White (13)
Diss High School, Diss

The Serpent

Haiku poetry

First, blurred memories,
Hatching slowly, carefully,
Freedom beckoned me.

Soon, I left the nest,
Trying to set in motion,
An easy future.

Then, he came to me,
The man with stark, white features,
And blazing red eyes.

I was there for him,
Every moment spent with his,
Sharing his whole life.

And then he did it,
Attacked the school he had loved,
The final battle.

I was so confused,
I didn't see it coming,
A clean, shining blade.

As I left this world,
I thought of one thing alone.
My name's Nagini.

Laurie Shaw (11)
Diss High School, Diss

26

Marcus Stroman

When the ball flies your way
There is only one way to stop it,
Hit it.

In the next inning
They get ready for play,
Jays have a talk
To improve their play.
Then the manager makes the call,
Stroman's up to play!

He stands staring
At the glove,
He pulls back his arm,
He lets go.

After the big game
Marcus gets the call,
The team are now sad,
The call is from The Mets,
They want Stroman.

Now he plays for the NY Mets,
But it is quite clear,
That deep down,
His heart is in Blue Jays!

Hamish Teare (12)
Diss High School, Diss

Being A Teen

I cried myself to sleep again,
Trying to hide the constant pain,
Not just from someone,
But from everyone.
I placed clothes upon my fragile skin,
To hide the sorrow which lies within,
I pulled the mask against my cheeks,
To hide the pain, that's been building for weeks.

I walked myself to school,
Walked past all of the cruel,
And met up with my acquaintance.
We walked towards the entrance,
I smiled at people who walked past.
Knowing my smile will never last,
Just for now I'll just say,
That I will always be 'okay'.

Gracie King (11)
Diss High School, Diss

Welcome To The Web

I'm sitting on a building,
Waiting in the breeze,
For a robbery to occur.
It's boring until there's a crime,
Yes! Let's go.
Swing side to side,
Building to building.
Oh no! King Pin!
Let's take him down.
It's tough being Spider-Man.
Me and my friends always come together,
To play video games.
Then my spidey-senses tingle - crime!
I get excused and then go to the crime scene.
It was worse than I thought.
It
Was
Nothing. It was nothing.
All that for nothing.
Well, my day was bad.

Aidan Patrick Quinnan (11)
Diss High School, Diss

Darkness

I feel alone.
To him, my thoughts and feelings are unknown.
His obsidian black suit sleeps on his body,
My antiquated dress cries for new,
Somebody.
You slap me to the foreboding ground,
Your derelict words are so profound.
I must leave the man who uses my dreams,
From the present to the past, nothing gleams.
A pill to numb the mind,
I'm held unpleasantly behind.
Trapped.
I am a lead ready to be unattached.
He couldn't stop at one sip,
That sky bleeds darkness,
A cut grows on my bruised lip.

Tia Reed-Hall (12)
Diss High School, Diss

Mr West Ham

As I wake up on a Saturday morning,
I hear that the cockneys are calling.

I jump out of bed and go to the ground,
This is where I love to be, right here with the crowd.

As the game starts, I'm the first one out,
Clapping to the fans, they always let their hearts out.

I love this club, I've been here for fifteen years,
And I plan to stay here for many more years.

Whether it's player or manager, I don't care,
I just love it when I hear that bubbles fly everywhere.

Solomon Marcks (13)
Diss High School, Diss

Me In Captivity

I thought I was young.
I thought I was free.
But poor old me, not in a tree.
My natural home, gone, overgrown,
Now it's just me, sad and alone,
The only expression I can make,
Is a frown the size of my face,
Now it's just me in captivity.

There is no way of coming home.
It feels like I'm stuck under a dome.
My house is on fire.
My family is dead.
I'm just a monkey,
Who has no home.
Now I'm stuck here all alone.
It's just me in captivity.

Ellie Victoria Mitchell (11)
Diss High School, Diss

The Little Turtle

I'm a little turtle swimming through the sea,
it used to be my home, but now it's a battlefield.
It has been taken over by plastic.
My mum was just going to get some jellyfish for tea,
and saw one, but she didn't know it was a plastic bag.
It choked her until she died.
I had to watch this.
I just wish that plastic didn't exist.
I now have no one, and have to be careful,
or I will be with my mum.
Please, please stop pollution,
or my mum won't be the only one!

George Alexander McCathie (11)
Diss High School, Diss

As I Hunt My Prey

Darkness surrounded me,
As I silently stalk my prey,
The wind whistled through my fur,
One wrong move,
And all could be lost.
I crept through the long grass,
I was getting close,
As I could hear faint squeaking,
It's beady eyes darted around,
Yet, still,
Was unaware of my presence,
Tiny droplets of water fell upon me,
A deep growl came from the sky,
Suddenly,
A blinding,
Jagged light bolted from the sky,
And the small rodent ran away.

Hallee Mai Watson (11)
Diss High School, Diss

The Hated Pizza Topping

Why am I so hated?
Put down and left in
The cupboard with
Stinky cheese and mouldy crackers.
I'm left crying in a corner.

Why am I so gross,
And disgusting? I don't get it.
I'm the sweetest fruit
You could ever have.
Just when will I taste nice?

Why was I born a pineapple?
My yellow texture makes
Me look sickening and my stem
Is sharp and hard to hold on,
As they are spiky and dumb.

Why was I born a pineapple...

Owen Holmes (11)
Diss High School, Diss

Dreading The Day

Hello.
There are a few days to go.
The day some love.
The day some dread.
But especially, for me, the day when I get stood on the head.
Saturday is the kick-off day.
The time when the other team must pay.
Lost match, we didn't gain.
But this time we'll give them some pain.
You think, who am I?
A football hooligan?
No, a matchday pie?
What are you thinking?
I'm the guy where the match gets played.
I'm the stadium.

Logan Cobb (13)
Diss High School, Diss

The Concert

Ed Sheeran

It's gone by so fast like lightning,
It's gone from clubs to busking fun, and now this.
The biggest day of my life, it's finally time.
Here I am, on stage, Divide tour,
All around the world I go,
Country to country, city to city.
I stand there on the stage,
Crowd screaming, crowd crying,
And crowd clapping for me.
Nervously standing there,
I strum my guitar,
I open my mouth
And the words flow out.

Katie Weedon (12)
Diss High School, Diss

Difference

We all stepped on this Earth at the same time,
So how are we different?
This Earth was made for all of us, not some of us.
We are separated by a gate and an army,
Does it have to be this way?
Why can't we be united, or was it planned this way?
Thousands of us shut away, no one caring what we say.
I died yesterday and thrown away
Like I was rubbish.
Why does it have to be this way?
Why?
Why?
Why?

Alfie Burr (12)
Diss High School, Diss

I Am Marmite

Hello, I am Marmite,
I'm that little tub inside your cabinet.
Me and you have a love-hate relationship.
You love me sometimes, but mostly you hate me.
Please don't confuse me with Nutella.
I'm not like Cinderella, I'm just a stinker,
Some people say I taste extremely salty.
But I can't help it, you tried me once,
And locked me up in the cabinet.
I am Marmite.
Love and hate me, I am right.

Gabriella Valcsak (12)
Diss High School, Diss

Love Of My Life!

I soared through the sky,
To save the one that caught my eye.

My heart paced back and forth,
As I was heading North.

Once I saw the love of my life,
The sun beamed down to create light.

I fought for his life, even though,
I should be fighting for mine.

As I finished the fight,
A rainbow gleamed bright.

As I saved,
The love of my life.

Ava Niamh Etchells (11)
Diss High School, Diss

Life As A Bird

As I soar through the trees,
I can feel the gentle breeze,
The lake is shimmering below
The glimmering sun.
As I fly high into the sky below me
I can see fellow friends,
The hedgehog and duck.
I swoop down below me to see
The chickens in their coop.
I'm off again, flying in the gentle breeze,
I glimpse down to see a bee collecting pollen.

Holly Davey (11)
Diss High School, Diss

Help Me

I'm lonely.
Isolated.
Neglected.
No one likes me.
Nothing likes me.
Not even my cell-mate.
I feel cut off from the world.
An hour feels like a day,
A day feels like a week,
A week feels like a month,
A month feels like a year.
I've got no memories of anything that has happened.
I have nothing to live for.
Help me!

Josh Amey (12)
Diss High School, Diss

My Life As A Teen

It's hard being a teen.
You feel trapped and insecure.
I get bullied and hurt.
I cry myself to sleep.
Step outside.
Feel ashamed.
Walk to school.
People laugh.
Run home.
Chuck my bag.
Run upstairs.
Grab my notebook.
Draw my feelings.
Picture of myself.
In a black room
It hurts me...

Ellie-Mae Blades (11)
Diss High School, Diss

The Prisoner

Lying on the squeaky, hard mattress,
I hear the prison guard's keys jingle.
The orange jumpsuits blinded me
As the moaning prisoners walked past.
Every day someone leaves,
I'm just waiting for my chance.
Sitting bored, waiting for my disgusting stale meal.
Nobody talks to me, as I'm known as the psychopath.

Amelia Smith (11)
Diss High School, Diss

Animals And Me

Animals are my friends,
Although some live in pens,
Exhilarated and excited they are,
As their imagination grow by for,
Animals and me,
We will be best friends forever,
And we'll always stick together,
Life is full of animals
And it always will be,
Because friendship is the key.

Tori Smith (11)
Diss High School, Diss

The Transition

The doors were so big,
I walked through them and smelt fig,
There was a feast,
Wow! It was big enough for a beast,
Teacher, students, candles for a ceiling,
I got this warm feeling,
My name is Harry Potter,
I am a wizard and I am proud.

Mia Worby (11)
Diss High School, Diss

The Unwanted Skater

I glisten in the sun like an invitation to play,
As you eagerly approach.
Your blades slice my skin,
As you laugh joyfully on me.
I get angry at your selfishness,
My body creaks,
Threatening to break,
Enveloping you into my icy soul.

Grace Henderson (12)
Diss High School, Diss

Through Jack Dawson's Eyes

The things I have seen,
It has scarred me,
The only luxury I have known,
Drowns before me.

Possessions and treasures,
Lost down at sea,
Now all my regrets,
Still, stick me with me.

A poor boy from Wisconsin,
Winning a bet,
Longing for a home.
No longer in debt.
Maybe there is hope.
A new life for me,
A chance to start over,
In the land of the free.

There she was,
On the edge,
Preparing to jump,
To her death.
I leapt over to save her,
I told her, "Don't do it."
She turned around,
She was beautiful,
I knew I could not quit.

Skip to the next day,
And we are in love,
Nothing can keep us at bay,
As angelic as a dove.

A scraping noise.
Water flooding through the hole.
Cherish me and all my joys,
Helpless as an orphan foal.
"Don't panic, please don't!"
Trying to calm people down,
Everybody shouted,
"We're going to drown!"

"Come on, Rose, we've got to go!
We need to jump!"
Water was our greatest foe.
My heart began to faster pump.
The ship is breaking,
Splitting in two.
"Rose, I want you to know
How much I love you!"
Avoid the water,
Have to survive,
Don't look back,
Just close your eyes.

I grabbed her arm,
We jumped off the ship,
Meaning no harm,
We took the dip.
Found an old door,
Helped her aboard,
Searched for an oar.
There go my dreams of living abroad.
It all went dark.
Don't know what happened next.
Everyone will remember that trip,
That ship,
But for me, it ended,
Jack Dawson. RIP.

Evie Newton (11)

Honley High School, Honley

Amelia Earhart

Up among the clouds, so clear and pure,
I fly, in an attempt to be the first woman to fly the Atlantic.
With adrenaline, plenty, I neared my goal,
I thought about my company, Loneliness, and how
It had served me on my trip.
I thought about family, friends and home.
I am oh so far from home.
I'm in a fortress of thoughts of my own but
As land stumbles into sight,
Immense thrill flooded through me.
Yes, I had done it.
I did it for America. I did it for my town.
I did it for my family.
I hope I will be remembered.
As my planes wheels stroked the ground gently,
I landed with accomplishments plenty.

Benjamin Crosland (11)
Honley High School, Honley

KSI

Starting with nothing,
Ending with fame,
Rising through the ranks of YouTube,
Glory to my name.

Starting with no experiences,
Wanting to try something new,
I'm going to rap and create songs,
I believe I will succeed.
Making top trending,
Achieving my goal.
This shows you if you believe and try,
You can do anything you want.
But if something goes wrong,
Don't give up,
Friends and family are there to help.

I wanted to be a professional boxer,
Now I am in the ring.
My fans behind me,
Encouraging me,
Since when I began.

Daniel Lydall (11)
Honley High School, Honley

Turtles

I'm fifty now, and I've seen a lot.
Half the coral has gone, destroyed by you.
Plastic is rapidly building up. There are piles of plastic under the sea.
The sea is getting warmer and warmer.
This is a major trauma.
I've been covered in plastic, I hate it, can you stop it?
You need to be on top of your game.
There is lots of beach to clean up.
Teach your friends and family to keep our planet clean.
We want to be here in years to come.
Make this planet bliss, help save us,
And all the other marine animals.
Save our planet now, think fast, before it's the end.

Holly MacGregor (11)
Honley High School, Honley

The Hunted

Soaring.
Soaring through the skies.
I'll someday stop.
I'll someday die.

Warm.
Cold.
Brilliant.
Emotions fill my head.

Flying.
Flying away.
Bullets.
Bullets passing my head.
Gunshots filling my ears.

Being hunted.
Hunted again.
Flying home to my lovely den.

Home.
Safe at last.
Relieved I didn't suffer consequences.
Of my discomfort.

Whilst I am here, in my cosy den.
All snuggled up tight.
Now, I will wait for the sunrise.
Before adventuring out to play again.

John Fox Gahan (11)
Honley High School, Honley

54

Adelle Tracey

I'm ready and waiting,
My adrenaline pumping,
At the start of the whistle,
I hear my heart thumping.

I set off at a pace,
That's as fast as a cheetah,
Through the darkest jungle,
Running wild and free.

Go faster and faster,
500 metres I'll achieve,
My mind stays focused,
I just need to believe.

Two people pass by me,
I feel the dread build inside.
I have to keep going,
As the end is in sight.

The finishing line
Appears before me,
Running for my life,
Fourth place is my fate.

Molly Eliza Clarke (11)
Honley High School, Honley

Sheep In The Mud

On a warm summer's night,
The glaring sun set,
I watch the fire crackle.

I sat with Jo in the mud,
Waited for Mamma to call.
The others walk by
Looking glum.

Out he came with the devil dog,
Into our field.
Sadness.

He came to give us a look,
Guilt.
He shooed me inside,
All I could do was hide.

I believe on that night,
Jo died.
Me a little sheepy,
Friend deprived.

Little did I know,
The next one was I.

Lexie Booth (12)
Honley High School, Honley

56

Looking Through The Eyes Of Lebron James!

I am Lebron.
All I can hear
Is loud cheers
And net slings,
Balls bouncing,
And crowds screaming.
Wait!
What was that?
We won!
Yay!
I can hear crowds clapping and celebrating,
And others booing at their loss.
Now comes the best part of the match,
The moment everyone has been waiting for,
The great trophy lifting!
As the sweat drips off of our heads,
And the ball stops bouncing at last,
The trophy gets lifted high,
And the curtains close.
Victory at last!

Dhaya Haire (11)
Honley High School, Honley

Rebecca Adlington - Competition Time

Heartbeat. *Boom. Boom. Boom.*
Deep breath.
Sweat. *Drip. Drop.*
Nerves.
Dread.
Hope...

Contestants.
Water.
Audience.
Eyes.
Camera.

Take your marks... Go!

Dive.
Legs.
Arms.
Determination.
Persistence.

One...
More...
Stroke...
Crowd goes wild!

Applause.
New personal best.
Achievement.

Happiness.
Congratulations!

Name.
Podium.
Medal.
Gold!

Best day ever!

Amber Eliza Dawson-Spragg (12)
Honley High School, Honley

Superman

There are times
When you think I am made of steel.
There are times
When you think I am indestructible.
There are times
When you think I am nowhere near human.
Anyone would think I couldn't be broken.
Anyone would think 'Wow!'
Wouldn't it be great to be a
Superhero, but not all heroes wear capes.
Yet, this one did.

He saw the problem.
He fixed the problem.

Superman.

He was everybody's hero,
Especially his own.

Eliza Faye Holroyd (11)
Honley High School, Honley

Paws

A big, wide world,
Under little eyes,
With miles and miles,
In the distance.

I look up into the dark
Sky and see how small,
I really am,
I stumble and I stamp,
Until I find my way
Home.

My paws are hurting,
And my legs are trembling,
But no small creatures gives
Up. I finally see home and
I shake off and go in.
I see the warm, cracking
Fire and go lay in
Front of it.
I get my belly rubbed,
And slowly fall asleep.

Isabella Pickup (11)
Honley High School, Honley

Billie Eilish

I sing and sing and sing.
I try my best to write songs
For my fans.

Country to country to country.
I do tours all over the world.

Practising, practising and practising.
I train my hardest so I can perform
An entertaining performance.

Meeting and meeting and meeting.
I meet lots of different people everywhere.

Showtime. Showtime. Showtime.
I wait for my time on stage.
The crowd roars and shouts for me
As I sing my heart out.

Molly Brannelly (11)
Honley High School, Honley

The Force

999, as I race to the scene,
Blues switched on, red
Lights no longer mean anything
To me.
My head spinning as I weave
Through traffic to get over there
ASAP.

What will I discover when I
Arrive at the incident?
Maybe damage?
Possibly aggression?
Or even injuries?
I'll have to find out,
My heart is racing,
What will I be facing?

I do this job every day,
To protect people,
And get them out of harm's way.

Declan Levay (11)
Honley High School, Honley

Replacement

Dying. Hard to breathe.
Every day
I see your talent.
You use me to create art.
Yet,
You are ready to throw me away.
Every day,
I think you're going to do it.

I am terrified.
How?
How can you bin me?
I help you make your art,
You need me!

There he is,
My replacement,
My life was short,
And yet I'm smiling.

Though I am scared,
I am happy.
Your art will continue,
Just without me.

Dylan Thomas Shaw (13)
Honley High School, Honley

Numb

Today is nothing.
A black dot in existence.
A numb expense where
The only sensation is pain.
I try to reach out, put on a smile,
Be happy but,
When I open my mouth,
The words escape me
Like a bird set out of its cage.
If only I could be set out of mine.
I'm held back by the chains of my insecurities,
They tighten every step I take.

I feel numb.
Just numb.

Omar Koroma (13)
Honley High School, Honley

England Cricket Team

I wonder what it's like winning the World Cup,
And drawing the Ashes.
It must have been dreadful for the Aussies
When Steve Smith hit the floor.
We were lucky to even get a draw.
Come on England! You can't stop here,
Or else this whole world will sneer.
Especially if you've got Jofra bowling
At ninety miles per hour!
The Mighty Lions are ruling with power.

Charlie David Shaw (11)
Honley High School, Honley

Pewdiepie Life

I started from the bottom,
Making videos 'till one hundred.

Making lots of content 'till five-hundred.

Getting lots of money,
Getting more views.

Soon hitting thousands,
Then hitting millions.

Getting lots of achievements,
From Youtube.

Then hitting my dream goal,
Guess what it could be?

100,000,000!

Kane Eley (12)
Honley High School, Honley

My Grandad

I like watching the racing.
I like watching the football.
I can't wait to have something to eat.
I hope it is something nice.
Ah, where is my food?

Gosh, I need some food.
The football is going to be on soon.
Come on.
Go on. Go on, score the goal.
Why did they do that?
They had an opportunity then.

Jessica Lilley (12)
Honley High School, Honley

Tesla

Fast, sleek and so much more,
The car is just to adore.
Go at night, drive at day,
It wants you to have a big day.
From zero to sixty in just four,
For you to have so much more.
The car is beautiful, and amazing,
It always keeps the fans gazing.
Without emitting a single fume,
It saves the world from big gloom.

Yousaf Umar Aziz (11)
Honley High School, Honley

Butterfly

Everything's so big.
Everything's so low.
My wings are so delicate.
Grass as long as hay.
My wings are as colourful as paint.
I go flower to flower,
Red rose, blue violets,
All colourful too.
My life has just begun,
My days are far from done.
It's time to go.
Leaving my fluttery flow.

Anayat Yaseen (12)
Honley High School, Honley

Around The World

The chimes and sounds of the old Greek church.
The deep dark woods filled with oak and birch.
The hot sunny deserts of Texas, USA.
The April showers in February and May.
Oranges growing on Spanish trees.
In London, scones with jam and cream.
Life in Africa, in the Sahara,
Lions, hippos and stripy zebras.

Emily Grace Bradley (11)
Honley High School, Honley

My Sausage Dog

Everything is so close.
Big.
Beautiful.
Wait, where's my bum?
Is it still there?
Oh, wait, there is my tail.
It's still there, yes.
Step. Step. Step. Step.
There's my food.
Yes!
A treat!
Oh no! The cat's there.
I need to hide.
Where can I go?
Um...
Ball!

Emily Lowther (12)
Honley High School, Honley

Through

Cold. Dark. Painful.
Loneliness. Helplessness. Powerlessness.
No one is here for me.

All alone in the world,
Crying inside.
I see nothing.
I feel nothing but pain.

I want to be free.
I want to break free.
I feel low.
I feel disappointed.
I feel like giving up.

Amber Nelmes (13)
Honley High School, Honley

Endangered Grassland

How would you feel,
Your family, gone,
Little food,
Safety - none,
Poachers in my grassland,
Loaded guns in their hands.

How would you feel,
Being hunted for ivory,
Hunted out of existence, gradually,
No food,
No family,
No safety,
Our species gone.

Leo Jackson (12)
Honley High School, Honley

Into The Light

Nervous. Excited. Enthusiastic.
Waiting behind the curtains,
The crowd roaring like lions,
As I stepped into the light,
Oh, wow! What a sight.
It was overwhelming
That there were so many people I could see,
Were they all chanting for me?
It's my time to shine.

Khiara Delgado (11)
Honley High School, Honley

Kung-Fu Panda

I am black and white, with a hint of brown.
Let me be free to eat my green tree.
Save me from those human beings.
I don't want to be extinct.
You will never find me when I'm asleep.

I have stared in so many movies.
I'm Kung-Fu Panda.

Ruben Christopher Charles Harrison (11)
Honley High School, Honley

Through The Eyes Of A Horse

Over walls.
Over hedges.
Over fences.

Eating grass.
Eating hay.
Eating grain.

Eating.
Sleeping.
And running around.
All day, every day.

Sleeping in fields.
Sleeping on straw.
Sleeping in or out.

Eva Tilburn (12)
Honley High School, Honley

Chicken

Massive.
So big.
Why is everything so big?
Cold, oh so cold.
This massive world is so cold.
Good, oh so good.
This food is so good.
So cosy, oh so warm.
This bed is so warm.

Alex Szoradi (11)
Honley High School, Honley

The Eye Of Thunder

A man walking down the simple, build road,
Even walking in the thundery cove.
Yes, the wind was strong,
But luckily not that long.
The wind stopped and perished out of the sky,
The man jumped and cried,
Tears of joy, touching the ground,
Sitting waiting for a frown.
But then, now the thunder hit,
He had no umbrella or even a tip.
As he looked up without a hood,
An eye coming out the sky far and wide,
Sat there, it started, eye on no side.
It came closer and made it night,
It took the man with a fright,
The thing took him and said,
"Beware the Eye of Thunder
Or this will be you next."

Faith Murphy Jones (11)
Savio Salesian College, Bootle

Orangutan

O ur homes, gone in seconds.
R uining our lives.
A lways finding somewhere new.
N obody thinks about us.
G radually less and less trees for
U s to live in.
T oo much for me
A nd the other orangutans,
N o one realises.

Selena Anderson (11)
Savio Salesian College, Bootle

Dina Asher-Smith

I was sitting on the sofa watching my hero,
Then I said to my mum,
"That'll be me."
Soon later, I was scouted by a coach,
My parents supported me very much.

Now I'm here at the 2019 World Championships,
Breaking records,
Winning medals,
Doing things I never thought I could.
Got a silver in the 100m,
Because I trained and trained to achieve my goal,
But is this a dream, I don't know.

The 200m came and went,
It had appeared I'd come first in the event,
The commentator had shouted once again,
"It's Dina Asher-Smith!"
These words just felt familiar,
Then the 4x400m relay, I won a silver.

The two silver and one gold medal of which I thought was a
dream,
Actually appeared to be real,
Emotion rushed through my body,
I had done it for everyone.
Everyone who had supported me.
Everyone who had helped me to achieve my dream.

Ameera Aslam (11)
The Oldham Academy North, Royton

Mummifying Nature

Chopping away at my roots to busy to know,
My motherhood of nature begins to slow.
Never taking in a moment of what harm is being caused,
You just sigh, then carry on with a cause.
I am here, you know, I can feel,
Stabbing me in the back like a seal.

I am an ocean of trees, where the wind goes,
Earth's beauties
Where the howling wind blows,
The poppies in the fields,
The birds in the sky,
The fish in the sea,
Let me be.
I am tired, stop cutting the trees,
Stop making fires, you're killing the bees.

I am a tree,
I am the moors,
I am a hill,
I am the grass,
I am everything you see
That is the colour of the sea.

Polluting my insides with poisonous fumes,
You leave me in distraughtness
And burn me to the side of a pea.

Poseidon, Poseidon, God of the Sea,
Cleanse me from this illness and let me be free.
I adore your love, providing me with a tsunami of hugs,
Envelope me with your kindness and be my little cub.

Grateful, I am, for ridding me to be clean,
Although I have to confess,
I yearn for your aura,
I am no longer mean!

Cheryl Brown (11)
The Oldham Academy North, Royton

Pretentious

An owl, wise, the mark of Athena,
A nocturnal being, as perfect as Angelina.
What about a courageous tiger?
I could be mighty, a fearless fighter,
I could be a French lady, ooh la la,
Rich without fears and all my lar die das!
What about mother saying, "Be proud of your identity."
But I can't. I just can't, it isn't in my mentality.
It's what I grew up with, racism, "Hey you! You don't belong here!"
I was alone, with no one, just my fears.
I wanted to be white, a hero, a celebrity.
Later I learnt all I need is my own integrity.
It's what you are, your personality, that counts.
Don't let haters victimise and pounce.
You are you, who you are meant to be.
I am me and I will never, from haters, flee.
Don't blame yourself, it is disastrous.
I have just one piece of advice.
Stop being pretentious.

Moezza Asad (13)
The Oldham Academy North, Royton

You Will Win

Background equals chance of success,
Is that correct or is it just a lie?
Will your life turn out a mess?
Will it all end in sighs?

Peer pressure, opportunities, time to grow
All lost because of your status low
But you can change this only you,
By being true to yourself, keeping the truth,
Start now, begin from youth,
As only you can change this, only you.

Don't listen to anyone else,
As this is your life, your time to strive
Block out all the people,
Block out all the noise,
And as long as you try, you will be fine.

Background equals change chance of success
Is that the truth or is it a lie?
Will your life turn out a mess?
Will it all end in sighs?

You can be successful,
You can win,
You can do this,
You will win!

Sharmin Akthar (13)
The Oldham Academy North, Royton

Silent, Lonely

Silent, lonely,
Darkness consumed me.
Invisible, depressed,
I observe the happiness avoiding me.
Fearful, isolated,
Tears stream down my face.
Sorrowful, downcast,
Dejection devoured my soul.

Distressed, resentful,
If we could only turn back time.
Scarred, traumatised,
The moment of my downfall could've been avoided.
Helpless, hopeless,
They don't care about me.

Guilty, guilty,
It's all my fault.
Resentful, ashamed,
I allowed myself to drown in sorrow.
Useless, pathetic,
I didn't deserve any happiness.
Unwanted, rejected,
I had pushed everyone away from me.
Worthless, disgusted,
Nothing could fix me.

Joyless, irreparable,
Defeated, irremediable,
Silent, lonely...

Masuda Begum (13)

The Oldham Academy North, Royton

I Was There

Me.
No, It.
The thing that lives outside of me.
It tired my neck by its integrity.
Me, its copy.
Me, its clone.
Me, its slave but forever alone.
But forever we are one,
Inseparable, undone.
It only sees me in the light,
And by these invisible chains, I can't fight.
But what it doesn't know is that
I was there.
When it's dark
I stand and stare,
In its secret places, I'm aware
Of the bad.
The end is near
And then it will know
I've seen it all,
And what's sown is sown,
When God is there.
On his pigment throne.

Yes, it shall know,
That I was there.
Yes, it shall know,
That I was there.
Yes, it shall know,
That I was there.

Favour Eguasa (13)
The Oldham Academy North, Royton

Climate Change

The Earth is heating up,
And we don't seem to care.
Electricity, fuel, litter,
Things I can't seem to bare!
We are making the Earth sick,
Seeing the weather have a range.
We don't want this anymore,
I want the world to change!
"You must be the change you wish to see in the world."
Quotes Mahatma Ghandi.
People die every day,
And could be one of your family.
The Amazon Rainforest has been burnt down.
The lungs of the Earth have been destroyed.
And unfortunately,
Some just seemed to avoid.
Hi! My name is Anisha,
And I need you.
Because the Earth is heating up,
So, people, you need to come through!

Anisha Saeed (13)
The Oldham Academy North, Royton

The Kidnapper

Every day goes past, but no one comes.
Weeks go past, but still no one comes.
Months go past, but no one comes.
Finally, every once a year, someone comes,
But they come to kill and kidnap,
But not me.
As a wretched human comes along my branches light up,
But as they go again, my branches droop.
No one comes to visit.
No one comes to stay.
But one day, out of the blue, a human comes,
With a massive tool and hacks away,
Creating bruises along my leg.
Hurting me.
But no one cares.
I crash to the ground, he drags me along.
Chucks me in a van.
I realise it was the end.

Iza Kauser (11)
The Oldham Academy North, Royton

We All Die

I'm suffocating.
Love is my air.
Hate is my H2O.
I'm drowning.
Life isn't fair.
We all die.

Left, right, left, right,
My trench space is tight.
Soldiers can't bring love,
Only hate.
Eventually, we all suffocate.
We all die.

Old before my time,
I enter no man's land.
Five heads up, run!
People soon die by the gun.
We all die.

His finger's on the trigger,
But the trigger's finger is mine,
One day everything will be fine.
Or maybe not,
We all die.

Fahmida Begum
The Oldham Academy North, Royton

Destiny

Who are we? What is this?
Is it real, or am I just imagining this?
Is it a dream or is it a nightmare?
Who are we and what's coming next?
None of us know who we truly are.
We know our past, we know out present,
But we don't know our future.
Do we really have friends, or is it just an act?
It's like a trap, once you're in there's no getting out.
Life. What happens next? Is it a choice or is it just fate?
Can we change where we will be?
Or is it just destiny?
Who are we and what's coming next?

Masuma Begum (13)
The Oldham Academy North, Royton

The Planet Complains!

I am a tree,
I am the green that you see,
Producing oxygen,
And giving shade,
From that sun you see shining down,
It's what I do,
But no one cares about me,
I see you play in the parks,
I see you grow,
I see you achieve your dreams,
I see your grave under me,
Lying down peacefully,
But then they chop me down,
Like I don't have a life,
But I do have a life,
In my way, in my language,
And every year I see five billion
Of my friends chopped down.
Is this really the end of me?

Ubaid Ullah Sharif Ali-Shanawar (11)
The Oldham Academy North, Royton

Future Eyes

When I was ten I did not know
About the power, I have now.
I got locked up because I am dangerous,
But I made a friend who I love.
She is kind, caring and funny,
I love her like family.
But I shouldn't have looked into her eyes.
But I couldn't help it, I looked into them,
And saw the beautiful future
We have together, and she was an auntie
When we are older, because she is
Like a sister to me.
And I don't want to live here forever,
Because she is my best friend.

Ashleigh-Tashan Alexis Howes (12)
The Oldham Academy North, Royton

El Chapo

I tried to shout,
But there was no one here.
I tried to scream,
But no one would listen.

I try to talk,
But I always sound drunk,
But that is how life works.

One day, I screamed for help,
But someone listened,
Who was it?

I turned around faster than a cheetah,
Slower than a plane,
But there I saw freedom.

I jumped higher than a kangaroo,
And turned skinnier than a bat.

There was the window,
That would take me to freedom.

Mehedee Hasan Rana (14)
The Oldham Academy North, Royton

Shot Dead

I curled up in the corner, shivering and cold.
Gunshots and screams, my heart turns to stone.
Father promises he'll be back, I wait every day.
More and more men are being taken away.

I work for hours for people who have no meaning to me.
They pay me little, I barely have enough to eat.
Locked up in the cellar, gloomy and cold.
Torture and violence, they will never get old.

Cookery and slavery are my jobs today.
I have no meaning in this world, but working for the
wealthy.

Myiesha Hussain (11)
The Oldham Academy North, Royton

How Would You Feel?

How would you feel if each of your arms fell,
One by one?
How would you feel if where you were living
Started to seem like Hell?
How would you feel if you were being set alight
Each and every night?
If your sky turned black, filled with smoke
And made you choke?
How would you feel if all of your friends were to disappear,
Lost forever and full of fear?
Now you know how I feel,
Because all of this seems too real,
So please help me to be fire-free.
#SaveTheAmazon

Sophia O'Brien (12)
The Oldham Academy North, Royton

Losing You

Three years ago,
You left me today.
A Saturday,
That changed my life in a weird way.

Slowly,
Things fell apart.
My mood declined off the charts.

I was sad,
But smiled at times,
Which made me feel really bad.

How did I manage to cope?
I had hope.
That one day,
I could see you,
Hug you,
Have a moment to talk to you,
Even make you a brew.
I miss you.

Lailah Rahman (13)
The Oldham Academy North, Royton

The Bully

I stay quiet, keep myself to myself,
I really don't think that's good for my health.
I wish you could feel this pain inside,
It doesn't go away, I should know, I've tried.

I take each day as it comes,
Sometimes I sleep because it numbs,
Every day I go to school,
I always get home with a bruise.

They try to act cool,
Just to make me look like a fool,
I wish they could see,
The damage they do to me.

Caitlin Monk (12)
The Oldham Academy North, Royton

My Worries

I'm a celebrity, a sportsperson and a TV star.
These are my hobbies,
But I don't enjoy them as much as I used to.
With all the pressure holding me down,
I want to drown.

With one goal they all give me the ball to score.
One minor mistake, brings me all the way down,
To give me a very big frown.

And when I go out my house,
It's a really big over-crowd
But that's all right, it gives me the crown.

Idrees Saddique (11)
The Oldham Academy North, Royton

Peer Pressure

The voices grew louder,
And the world muted,
"Do it. Do it. Do it."
But I didn't want to,
I didn't have to,
I knew this,
But I gave in,
Threw all my dignity in the bin.

Why did I go through with this?
This is such a mess,
Now I have to deal with the stress
Lying on the floor, so numb,
Why am I so dumb?
I didn't want to,
I didn't have to,
But I gave in.

Alisha Maybury (13)
The Oldham Academy North, Royton

Where Am I?

I hope I will be able to feel the
Winter's bitter breeze or the warm summer air.
Why didn't I ever say I love you?
Why did I ever leave you?

I wonder will you ever find love again?
Will I? What, am I kidding? I'm dead,
Deader than this roadkill.

I wish I could feel the soft touch of your skin,
and see the shine of your emerald green eyes.

I hope I can see you again.

Donovan Drew Thistleton (14)
The Oldham Academy North, Royton

The Ocean

The world doesn't care about me,
I just want to live and be free.

But unfortunately, I can't,
The junk the humans are throwing into me is like
A bad virus wanting to kill me.

But they've made a mistake,
I can build a terrible disaster
Which can end your life on Earth.
Now they can't repopulate or give birth
To the humans who are killing me.

This will be the end.

Mohammed Fahim Hussain (11)
The Oldham Academy North, Royton

BFF

How could she betray me like this?
We've known each other since we were little kids.
I thought we were BFFs forever.
I can't believe she'd betray me like this, not ever.

Days have gone by,
She still hasn't apologised,
I have to move on,
Forget and leave it all behind.

Be careful with who you trust.
They might turn their back,
Walk away, just brush you away
Just like dust.

Samiha Begum (13)
The Oldham Academy North, Royton

I Am Emmett Till

I am Emmett Till,
And I was born in a time when it was acceptable to kill.
I was lynched in 1945,
For just the colour of my skin,
Which didn't keep me alive,
For whistling to a woman,
Who wasn't even my race.
I was lynched, but I didn't even look her in the face.
I am Emmett Till,
And I was born in a time when it was acceptable to kill.

Jessica Nicole Meggison (14)
The Oldham Academy North, Royton

Siblings

Listen, I've got to tell
You a story about
A brother and his
Sister. They always
Supported each other
With the promise this
Love would last forever
And ever.

'Cause they shared
A love like no other,
Making sacrifices
For each other,
'Cause they go by:
'We're in this
Together!'

Atiyah Begum (13)
The Oldham Academy North, Royton

War

Sweat and blood
Dripping down my body,
A continuous stream.
Anger and determination,
Fills our eyes.
Dirty, cold skies,
Seem to strike down disappointment.
Death and slaughter,
Innocent men dying.
Heavy armour and weapons,
Weigh us down to our knees.
Forgive us, God,
For our terrible deeds.

Ryan Cropper (11)
The Oldham Academy North, Royton

Jesus, The Gift From God

Jesus, the gift from God.
Jesus, running down the wing.
Jesus, control, kick, kick *bang*!
Jesus, scoring goals every shot he takes.
Jesus, the gift from God.
Jesus, came down to win.
Jesus, control, kick, kick, *bang*!
Jesus, can you truly beat him?

Luke Hesford (13)
The Oldham Academy North, Royton

Peace

I opened my eyes,
I could hear cries,
A beautiful, warming smile from my mum,
There is was,
My home sweet home,
Oh, look at the sky,
Even so high,
The trees were swishing and swaying,
People were praying,
The Earth was peaceful.

Shobnam Yeasmine (11)
The Oldham Academy North, Royton

I Miss You

I really miss you
I had your favourite meal today
Even though I don't like vegetables
I still ate it all
I really miss you
I hope you're okay
How are your mum and dad?
Everyone misses you
Especially me
See you soon.

Jacob Houghton (11)
The Oldham Academy North, Royton

Families

Families are big
Families are small
But I love them all
Some have mothers
Some have fathers
And some have sisters
Some have brothers
I love them all
Some are pretty
Some are not
But that's why there are a lot.

Mia Broadbent (11)
The Oldham Academy North, Royton

Every Day I See...

Every day I see,
Bushes bustling,
Leaves hovering,
Dogs barking,
Cats running,
Vines hustling,
Frogs jumping,
Deers fleeing,
Mosquitos buzzing,
Chimpanzees laughing,
Birds chirping.

Kaif Zahir (11)
The Oldham Academy North, Royton

The Lonely Moon

I'm all alone.
I am lonely.
I am the one and only.
I'm the one created to reflect light
So people can see at night,
On the ground or on a flight.

Sami Chohan (12)
The Oldham Academy North, Royton

This Is What's Real

This made me look back into my heartbreaking past,
As my days go by, oh how I wish it was my last.
My brain is overflowing, overflowing of stress,
My heart is crying out to me why have the good days left.
Does the colour of my skin affect who I am?
Why does racism exist?

As I walk through the school hallways,
people point and laugh.
Why does this keep happening to me?
I ask...
I feel like in prison,
Why does racism exist?
This question is just on repeat in my head,
I wish I could just hide under my bed.
I'm drowning in complete utter stress.

The truth hurts but this is what's real,
As I sit here and I write I'm saying how I feel
I was a prisoner in racism's world
And I'm letting my feelings out
To all the people that hate and laugh.

This is a new start for me,
So please let me be.
I just want to be like all the people in the world,
Who have now been set free,
And are able to spread their wings and believe.

Kadija Diallo
Walton High, Walnut Tree

The Missing Bear

Today's a very missing day,
There's missing in the air.
Who is it could be missing?
Missing is the missing bear.

Who am I, you wonder?
You'll know right very soon,
Quick now me - I have to be,
I disappear full moon.

I'm running out, I'm running out,
Of precious, precious time.
Here's the bit, O here's the bit
That clearly doesn't rhyme.

"Who's the missing bear?
Who are you?
Are you the bear?
Are you missing?"

Well, how can I be missing,
When you know where I am?
Well, you are not so clever,
As you don't know my plan!

"I am not so stupid,
I'm a spirit hunter you see,
I've caught you now,
Which shows I persevere."

Time is so dangerous,
It's an unpredictable ground,
If you do not come with me,
You won't be safe and sound.

Oh, wise, courageous hunter,
Oh, spirit hunter I see,
You are just so silly,
You're being tricked by me.

"I know this world is dangerous,
But I won't come with you,
I know I won't survive,
But I won't die with you."

George Lashbrook (11)
Walton High, Walnut Tree

The Near Future

Oh dear! The future is near.
A chapter is closing: a new one is opening.
I know I should move on, but I can't forget what has gone
on,
It felt like yesterday when I left all my friends,
I can't forget that we were all sparkling gems.

Oh dear! The future is near.
Do I aspire to be like Anne Frank or Coco Chanel,
Or JK Rowling, or even myself?

In the near future will cars fly?
Will they take me sky-high?
Will I be able to breathe in space,
Without a mask but by using my face?
Using my face to smile and say hi,
To all the aliens which hopefully will reply.

In the near future will technology expand?
Will there be flying robots?
Will they listen to my commands?
Can people mind read in this near future?
Or can magic really be real?
Will Santa show up in my house, or will I hear reindeer land
on my roof?

In the near future will my dreams come true?
Will I be able to fly over the moon?
I'm guessing this future won't come very soon,
It'll take a lot of work,
But hey, this is between me and you!

Divya Vasisht (11)
Walton High, Walnut Tree

The Clown In The Bookcase

It was the day my life changed,
The day I faced my fear was arranged,
December 1st 1922.
I didn't want it, would you?
A book, an oh so scary book,
About a clown, oh the look
My nan gave me when I opened it up.
That birthday wasn't so fun.
I sat on my bed and looked at the cover,
Don't get me wrong, I'm a big lover
Of scary things.
I shoved it to the back of my bookshelf
And screamed.
I let out a gasp.
I let out a cry,
As it climbed to its feet on the carpet
And sighed.
It was a clown, whispering my name,
"Oh, Susy, don't be ashamed of yourself,
You let me free, now I shall kill you.
Let's see, would you like me to do something awful or
quick?"
I shuddered to think what he would do next.

Suddenly, I woke up.
3:20am. It was just a dream.
Then the book took to the floor,
Oh no, I thought.

Freyja Hawkins
Walton High, Walnut Tree

Untitled

I am a tree, I am going away
I have many friends but they're not here to stay
I've lost too much so I ran astray
To my safe place far, far away

I am the ocean, my strength is mighty
I am home to many but some are astray.
My strength being depleted by a thing called plastic,
I no longer think I am fantastic

I am the sun and I burn so bright
I am so bright I blind on sight,
I don't know how I'm being let in
It's way too much but hard to keep in

I am the Earth I once was bold
But now I'm starting to go so cold,
I burn with rage and freeze in sadness
No one can keep up with my badness

I am a human
I am a cause
I don't know why we haven't pressed pause,
I am the creator of all things bad
We need to *save everything*
So we can be glad.

Emily Cunningham (12)
Walton High, Walnut Tree

A Stranger's In My House

I fell asleep one night and heard voices in my head,
They told me that someone was downstairs,
But I knew those voices were fake.
I knew I was home alone,
So there should only be silence.
But the voices got louder and louder,
And the sound of footsteps got nearer and nearer.
I heard someone open a door.
As I opened my eyes I saw a shadow lying on the bed.
I closed my eyes and opened them again,
Hoping all would be gone,
But what filled my eyesight has given me nightmares ever since.
Bloodshot eyes stared directly into mine,
Long blond hair hung just at his neck,
His face, that was covered in blood, had no expression.
This figure stood still,
Still like a statue.
I had no escape...

Jenny Else
Walton High, Walnut Tree

Dear Diary

Anne Frank

Dear Diary, I'm locked up here, afraid, alone,
Chained and bound, I haven't eaten a scrap or bone,
I see no light, I have no home.
Help me, please, Dear Diary, I'm afraid, I'm alone.
Dad says we'll be out of here by tomorrow sunset,
I smile and listen but I have no hope yet.
I'm trapped, encaged,
Upset, enraged,
But that won't help me here.
I'm still quite young, but I've been put to work,
I'll wish and cry but the officers just smirk.
I need a wash, but my shower day is tomorrow.
Me, my friend and my family are going, but surprisingly not
Dad,
I saw him hiding the other day, what a silly man,
Well, anyway, see you tomorrow.
Yours sincerely, Anne.

Sophie Wright (11)
Walton High, Walnut Tree

Warriors

I looked at him as though he was an alien,
He called me,
I resisted the temptation to run away,
I am a warrior, not a coward who runs away.

He came closer,
I knew what he would do,
We've all heard the story of Graystripe,
How he was taken from his home,
By the Twolegs who destroyed the forest.

He came closer still,
I jumped back in alarm,
I heard barking,
The noise drew closer,
The yapping and snarling.

I pelted,
I heard them try to chase,
But their Twoleg kept them back,
I don't want to be here,
I want to go home,
Back to my nest,
I must go home,
To my nest,
Of warm moss,
Back to Thunderclan and the other cats.

Toby Atkinson (12)
Walton High, Walnut Tree

The Dissolving Love

The mother dog just gave birth,
To eight beautiful puppies,
She loved all of them,
But they got separated quicker,
Then they got to meet each other.

They all got sold off,
Each one to a different person,
But not all got as lucky,
As the rest.

Daisy, one of the puppies,
Got sold off to a small family,
Which seemed quite nice but,
The older Daisy got the
Less interest she got.

When Daisy was a puppy,
She looked really nice. She had,
Lovely hairstyles and a lot of love,
And attention.

But as she got older,
Her family didn't even
Notice her and barely
Took her on walks.

Oliwia Michalak
Walton High, Walnut Tree

To What Will Become

Death, destruction, damage,
If I cannot create love, I will cause fear,
The deep and direst cruelty
To what will become.

The murder,
The fear,
The sheer panic,
To what will become.

All because of the rejection,
Rejection from him,
Rejection from society,
To what will become.

This vile creature
Has more emotions than you know,
More power than you know,
To what will become.

This Demon, ugliness of a creature,
Will ruin your world,
Terrorise your surroundings,
The air of melancholy which will cause fear among victors.

To what will become.

Jemma Tye
Walton High, Walnut Tree

The Hunt

Every day is terror,
It's horrible for me.

No matter what the weather,
I always have to flee.

The whistles and howls,
They fill me with fear.

And the animal that growls,
Then tries to bite my ears.

My hole is getting nearer,
My mother, I can hear her.

But then it was clearer,
Never would I feel her.

My tail was in pain,
It was pouring with rain.

Then I felt the strain,
Like getting hit by a train.

Why, oh why, oh why,
Can't I live to see the sky?

Why, oh why, oh why,
Can't I live to see the sky?

Sam Alfie Mounch (12)
Walton High, Walnut Tree

A Day In The Life Of A Car

My owner every morning would unlock me.
He would get in.
He would start me up.
He would let me warm up.
He would drive me.
He would arrive at work.
I would sit there, having a nice nap.
Always ready to be driven again.
Just when I thought I'd be dead and rusted
He'd drive me to get my service done.
He'd never abuse me
And drive me home so I can be left alone.
Next morning, he'd do the same thing.
Except it was the weekend.
He'd arrive at the dealer.
And say goodbye to me as he drove off in another one.

David Garofil (11)
Walton High, Walnut Tree

The Day They Came

The day they came,
The ones to blame,
Are the ones who set this land aflame.
This is not a game,
They are not easy to tame,
All of our lives will never be the same.

The day they roared,
Houses were flooded,
And people cried to the one they called Lord.
Cries were ignored,
The land's in discord,
People died or ended up in a ward.

The day they kept,
The day they crept,
The day I couldn't dare to expect.
My sister was wrapped,
My father was strapped,
That was the day I would never accept.

Jorai Ngindu (13)
Walton High, Walnut Tree

Everybody's Missing

My dad has been killed.
My mum is ill.
My sister has been missing for days.
Oh, please help me, for goodness' sake.

Friends and family dying around me.
How sad my life is.
I have been kicked out of school
For not being clever.

Thousands of children not being educated.
How bad the future will be.
My mum wants the best for me,
I hope she never leaves.

Soon I will have to leave,
To go and fight for the country.
I hope I come back alive,
And make my mother proud.

Josh Wicks
Walton High, Walnut Tree

Sinking

As I sit in the cabin,
I feel my socks getting
Soggy.
I wonder what is going on...
I get up to see.
With each step, I almost get
Drowned
By the raging waves as they
Crash over me.
Terrified.
Was this a bad mistake?
I was scared, terrified,
Sick.
At this point, I just wanted to go
Home, but I knew I couldn't
The boat was sinking faster
I felt sick, like
Vomiting.
As the lightning struck,
It took a piece of the boat each time...
Was this the end?

Lizzy Ann Albans (11)
Walton High, Walnut Tree

Friends

We used to be friends,
But you know life bends.
I had happiness with her one day
But she had to grow up
And faded away.
She went from my sight
And even the light
My memory became dark
As if it were night.
I'm just a toy...
Is this my forgotten death?
No. Just take a breath
Now I think
She walked over and I blink
But then, she was gone
And I'm stuck here
Nothing be freed from
Shall I escape?
Oh, the choices I have to make.

Ella Smith
Walton High, Walnut Tree

In Front Of Me

All around me
I can see
My world demolishing
In front of me.

Nature is the key,
Flowers, grass and bees,
To help my world
In front of me.

The people are now too fancy,
With crackers and brie,
Buildings are taking up our world,
In front of me.

As an old oak tree,
I can see,
My world demolishing,
In front of me.

Naeya Mistry
Walton High, Walnut Tree

If I Could See What Is To Be

If I could see
What is to be,
The end of the trees,
The world on its knees,
I'd leave.
Go.
Die.
Find a predator, mash like a pie.
I am not shy,
But the future does terrify!
It makes you ask why;
Why the children will fry?
Why the children will have no planet?
Just a lifeless rock,
In the middle of a thoughtless world.

Fionnabhair Sarah Filer (13)
Walton High, Walnut Tree

Alone

They punch me, they
Tease me, they
Push and kick.
I am alone.
I talk to Mum
But she's too
Drunk to listen
And Dad, well,
He's dead.
I want to die;
I cut and bleed and cry.
The next day, no one
Knows yet,
But I've been
Wiped from Earth.

Shakima Nicholas
Walton High, Walnut Tree

Strangers

Pointing fingers
Shouting voices
Whines and horrifying screams
From every corner there is.
A cruel world
Built for horrible people.
Guilt
Blame
It's crushing.
And sadness
It's haunting every second.
An asylum that nobody escapes.

Ellie Gibson
Walton High, Walnut Tree

My Baton

B aton, that's my name.
A ll over my face is horrible sweaty hands.
T he amount of times I get chucked about is...
O utrageous.
N ever forget the amount of times I just drop to the floor!

Jessica Leeanne Edwards (12)
Wester Hailes Education Centre, Edinburgh

The Dancer

D ropping our baton isn't a big deal.
A mazing atmosphere.
N ever-ending cheering.
C ostumes irritating me.
E ffort is 100% right now.
R edder than a tomato.

Hannah Millar (11)
Wester Hailes Education Centre, Edinburgh

As I Stepped On The Floor

As I stepped on the floor,
I had butterflies.
My heart beating like a drum.
Everyone clapping is all I see from my eyes.

Emma Burt (12)
Wester Hailes Education Centre, Edinburgh

Teens

You don't feel like a teenager,
But you're one.
People tell you about your body,
But you don't listen.

Everyone grows up one day.
You can change in many ways.
You might fall over,
But that's okay.

Teens can already have a past,
But they can still have a future.
That doesn't matter,
One way or another.

Bullies in childhood,
Can still topple them down.
Fears of their past,
Can't scare them now.

Teens like to make a difference,
To be rebellious.
Start enjoying your life,
Or learn to achieve excellence.

So, what are teens?
Are they children?
Are they adults?
That doesn't matter at all.

Nina Petryk (13)
Wilmington Grammar School For Girls, Dartford

I Can Do This

I can do this.
What if I don't know anyone?
I can do this.
What if I'm running late?
I can do this.
What if I throw up?
I can do this.
What if I miss the plane?
I can do this.
What if the plane is running behind?
I can do this.
What if the plane crashes?
I can do this.
What if there is turbulence?
I can do this.
What if we miss the train?
I can do this.
What if I am all alone?
I can do this.
What if there is no one with me?
I can do this.
What if there aren't enough rooms?
I can do this!

Lucy Stapley (13)
Wilmington Grammar School For Girls, Dartford

Donald Trump

President of America.
Wants to build a wall
To keep the Mexicans out.
He's racist and a fool.
His appearance is bad.
He has an orange, blotchy tan.
Hair as yellow as a banana.
He's a bit of a strange man.
He rules the country.
Wants to start a nuclear war.
Nobody likes him.
He needs to grow up a little more.

Erin Gardner (13)
Wilmington Grammar School For Girls, Dartford

YOUNG WRITERS INFORMATION

We hope you have enjoyed reading this book – and that you will continue to in the coming years.

If you're a young writer who enjoys reading and creative writing, or the parent of an enthusiastic poet or story writer, do visit our website **www.youngwriters.co.uk**. Here you will find free competitions, workshops and games, as well as recommended reads, a poetry glossary and our blog. There's lots to keep budding writers motivated to write!

If you would like to order further copies of this book, or any of our other titles, then please give us a call or order via your online account.

Young Writers
Remus House
Coltsfoot Drive
Peterborough
PE2 9BF
(01733) 890066
info@youngwriters.co.uk

Join in the conversation!
Tips, news, giveaways and much more!

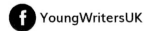